20 THINGS YOU DIDN'T KNOW ABOUT

EARTH'S RESOURCES

DOUG BRADLEY

PowerKiDS press

Published in 2023 by The Rosen Publishing Group, Inc.
2544 Clinton Street, Buffalo, NY 14224

Portions of this work were originally authored by Sarah Machajewski and published as *20 Fun Facts About Earth's Resources*. All new material in this edition was authored by Doug Bradley.

Editor: Greg Roza
Book Design: Tanya Dellaccio

Photo Credits: Cover pedrosala/Shutterstock.com; p. 5 Kletr/Shutterstock.com; p. 6 AlinaMD/Shutterstock.com; p. 7 GraphicsRF.com/Shutterstock.com; p. 8 GreSiStudio/Shutterstock.com; p. 9 3xy/Shutterstock.com; p. 10 robert dumitru/Shutterstock.com; p. 11 SkyLynx/Shutterstock.com; p. 12 (oil) Signature Message/Shutterstock.com; p. 12 (coal) Adam J/Shutterstock.com; p. 12 (gas) Licvin/Shutterstock.com; p. 13 1968/Shutterstock.com; p. 14 Jixin YU/Shutterstock.com; p. 15 ArtEvent ET/Shutterstock.com; p. 16 Henrik Lehnerer/Shutterstock.com; p. 17 syam fireshark/Shutterstock.com; p. 18 Aleksandr Pobedimskiy/Shuttertock.com; p. 19 Matej Kastelic/Shutterstock.com; p. 20 kryzhov/Shutterstock.com; p. 21 wawritto/Shutterstock.com; p. 22 (asprin) Hurst Photo/Shutteratock.com; p. 22 (willow bark) n_defender/Shutterstock.com; p. 23 Rich Carey/Shutterstock.com; p. 24 Jose de Jesus Churion Del/Shutterstock.com; p. 25 mavo/Shutterstock.com; p. 26 sergemi/Shutterstock.com; p. 27 (sun) Dmytro Balkhovitin/Shutterstock.com; p. 27 (waterfall) Maurizio De Mattei/Shutterstock.com; p. 27 (geyser) Puripat Lertpunyaroj/Shutterstock.com; p. 27 (logs) gkordus/Shutterstock.com; p. 27 (wind turbines) huang yi fei/Shutterstock.com; p. 29 Nejron Photo/Shutterstock.com.

Library of Congress Cataloging-in-Publication Data
Names: Bradley, Doug, author.
Title: 20 things you didn't know about Earth's resources / Doug Bradley.
Other titles: Twenty things you didn't know about Earth's resources
Description: Buffalo, New York : PowerKids Press, [2023] | Series: Did you know? earth science | Includes index.
Identifiers: LCCN 2022026211 (print) | LCCN 2022026212 (ebook) | ISBN 9781538389669 (library binding) | ISBN 9781538389645 (paperback) | ISBN 9781538389676 (ebook)
Subjects: LCSH: Natural resources–Juvenile literature.
Classification: LCC HC85 .B73 2023 (print) | LCC HC85 (ebook) | DDC 333.7–dc23/eng/20220808
LC record available at https://lccn.loc.gov/2022026211
LC ebook record available at https://lccn.loc.gov/2022026212

Manufactured in the United States of America

CPSIA Compliance Information: Batch #CWPK23. For Further Information contact Rosen Publishing at 1-800-237-9932.

CONTENTS

WHAT ARE NATURAL RESOURCES?

Earth provides us with many resources. Some natural resources, like the sun's heat, keep us alive. We also need air and water to survive. Plants and animals can't live in space because these things don't exist there. Some resources, such as rocks and **minerals**, are used for building. Many resources make our lives more enjoyable. We use gold to make jewelry. We use copper to make electrical wires.

All of these things are natural resources. They are materials found in nature that people use. Read on to learn some fascinating facts about Earth's resources.

Wood is another important natural resource that people use to make their lives better.

HERE COMES THE SUN!

DID YOU KNOW?

Light is the fastest thing in the universe... but it still takes eight minutes for the sun's light to reach Earth.

Most forms of life on our planet need sunlight to survive. This includes both plants and animals. Without the light and heat from the sun, Earth would be a cold, dark, lifeless place.

Energy from the sun is called solar energy.

PHOTOSYNTHESIS

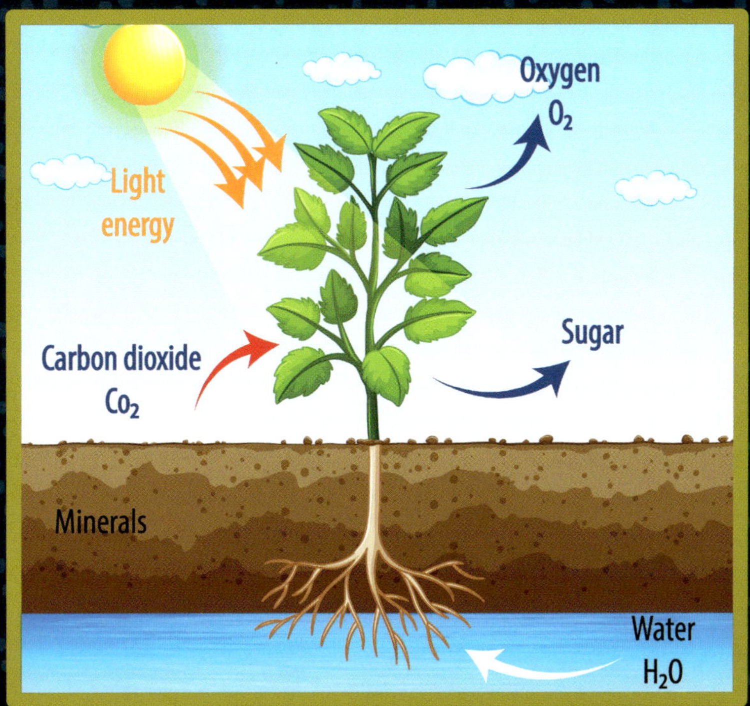

The food plants make is a sugar called glucose.

Most plants get their energy from sunlight and use it in a process called photosynthesis. Plants use sunlight, water, and a gas called carbon dioxide to make food during photosynthesis. Oxygen is a waste gas that plants give off during photosynthesis. All animals need oxygen to live!

DID YOU KNOW?

Plants need sunlight to make food.

EARTH'S WONDERFUL WATER CYCLE

DID YOU KNOW?

The water on Earth today is the same water that was on it millions of years ago.

Earth's water is always moving through a chain of steps called the water **cycle**. Evaporation is when water changes from a liquid to a gas. Condensation is when a gas cools and becomes liquid. Precipitation is when water falls out of clouds as rain or snow.

New water is never created, and water is never lost.

THE WATER CYCLE

THE POWER OF WIND

DID YOU KNOW?

People have been using wind power to do work for thousands of years.

The ancient Egyptians began using sails to power their ships on the Nile River around 5000 BCE. The first windmills were made around 200 BCE. Windmills have long been used to **pump** water out of the ground and grind grain.

A windmill, also called a wind turbine, is a machine that creates power as it spins. Wind pushes turbine blades and causes them to spin, creating power to do work.

In 2008, the town of Rock Port, Missouri, became the first U.S. community to be powered completely by wind turbines. Since then, many other U.S. communities have switched over to 100 percent wind power.

FOSSIL FUELS

DID YOU KNOW?

Fossil fuels take millions of years to form inside Earth.

Fossil fuels are really old—perhaps even 300 million years old! These sources of energy are made up of the broken-down remains from **organisms** that lived long ago.

Fossil fuels are found inside Earth's **crust**. They include coal, oil, and natural gas.

NATURAL GAS

OIL

COAL

After ancient plants died, layers of **sediment** slowly covered them. Over time, heat and weight turned the plants into coal. Today, coal contains the energy of those ancient plants.

DID YOU KNOW?

Burning fossil fuels releases the energy that plants originally collected from the sun millions of years ago.

Coal was discovered in China nearly 4,000 years ago.

Historians think this was the first time people burned a fossil fuel. Since then, coal has become one of the most used of Earth's natural resources. Coal is burned in furnaces to create heat. It is burned in power plants to create electricity.

China is still the world's top producer and user of coal. However, China is also the world leader in producing energy from renewable resources, such as solar, wind, and **hydroelectric** power.

DID YOU KNOW?

When burned, fossil fuels release **chemicals** that are harmful to living creatures.

Fossil fuels have long been used to power cars, trucks, motorcycles, buses, boats, and planes. They're also used to heat our homes and provide electricity. However, fossil fuels release dangerous chemicals when burned. These include carbon dioxide, **methane**, and **nitrous oxide**.

DID YOU KNOW?

The word "petroleum" comes from Latin words meaning "rock oil."

Crude oil, which is often called petroleum, is a thick, gooey liquid made of plant and animal remains. The word "petroleum" can also refer to natural gas, as well as a solid form known as bitumen.

Petroleum is made when organic matter piles up at the bottom of oceans and rivers and slowly changes over millions of years. Oil wells are created to find oil trapped under thick, solid layers of rock or clay.

Petroleum jelly has also been used as a skin moisturizer, hair-care product, diaper rash treatment, and more things.

DID YOU KNOW?

A **by-product** of petroleum mining is a clear "jelly" used for numerous self-care purposes.

In the 1850s, oil workers in Titusville, Pennsylvania, began using a clear jelly created by the oil-mining process to heal cuts and sunburns. Today, petroleum jelly is a common product in many households.

EARTH'S IRON

DID YOU KNOW?

Iron makes up a large amount of Earth's crust—about 6 percent.

Many important metals are mined from Earth's crust. One of the most important of these is iron. Rocks that have iron are called iron ore. They can be gray, rusty red, yellow, purple, or black.

Iron is an element that's found all over the planet—and deep inside it!

About 98 percent of the iron ore mined is used to make steel. Steel is a very strong metal that lasts for many years. It's used to make machines, tools, cars, trucks, and buildings, including skyscrapers!

HEALTHY SOIL

DID YOU KNOW?

Soil isn't just "dirt." It's a living, breathing home!

Soil is necessary for all kinds of life. Healthy soil is full of important **nutrients** and minerals. It filters, or cleans, our water and stores gases that we need to breathe. Many animals live in soil. Healthy soil helps healthy plants grow.

Healthy soil is very important to plants, animals, and people.

Earthworms are a sign that soil is healthy. The more worms, the healthier the soil! Earthworms dig through soil and create air pockets. They put important nutrients back into the soil. This helps plants grow.

PLANT POWER!

Plants give us many important **medicines.**

People have even been using plants to treat illnesses and make pain go away for thousands of years. Today, hundreds of plants are used to make medicines.

Long ago, people would chew on willow bark to ease pain. In 1897, the German company Bayer used willow bark to create the common pain-killing drug aspirin.

DID YOU KNOW?

Rain forests cover about 6 percent of Earth's surface.

Rain forests are home to over half the world's animal species and two-thirds of its plant species. They keep our water and air healthy and clean. They even affect Earth's weather patterns.

Fibers that come from plants are used to make most of the clothing you wear. Cotton and flax for linen are gathered and used to make shirts, pants, dresses, and more. Today, cotton is the plant that's most used to make clothing.

People all over the world have traditionally used weaving to create clothes, blankets, and more. Some people still use traditional weaving methods.

People have long used wood from trees to make homes, furniture, tools, ships, wagons, and much more. Today, carpenters use wood to build things including cabinets, fences, picnic tables, and even musical instruments.

RENEWABLE RESOURCES

DID YOU KNOW?

Renewable resources, such as wind, water, and sunlight, will never run out!

Renewable forms of energy creation are becoming more popular. These forms are better for Earth than the use of fossil fuels. That's because they won't run out and because they don't pollute the planet.

SUN

Geothermal energy is created by pumping water far enough underground that it is heated by Earth. This hot water can then be used to heat homes.

RENEWABLE RESOURCES

GEOTHERMAL

WATER

WOOD

WIND

SURVIVAL

Whether they're renewable or not, resources are necessary for human survival. We also depend on Earth's resources to improve our living conditions.

When we think about our planet's resources, it's important to remember that it's not just people who use them. We share our planet with plants and animals that need these resources to survive too. It's important to protect our natural resources so we can protect the future of Earth and its many organisms.

Rain forests are essential to all life on Earth. It's important to protect them and the plants and animals that call them home.

GLOSSARY

by-product: Something produced in addition to the main product.

chemical: Matter that can be mixed with other matter to cause changes.

crust: The top layer of Earth's land.

cycle: A series of steps that repeat over and over.

hydroelectric: Related to the production of electricity by water power.

medicine: A drug that a doctor gives you to help fight illness.

methane: A colorless, odorless gas that is a pollutant and greenhouse gas.

mineral: A naturally occurring solid substance that's not of plant or animal origin.

nitrous oxide: A colorless gas that is a pollutant and greenhouse gas.

nutrient: Something taken in by a plant or animal that helps it grow and stay healthy.

organism: An individual living thing.

pump: To use a tool, called a pump, to move water or gases through pipes.

sediment: Matter such as rocks, sand, and stones that's moved and deposited by water, wind, or glaciers.

FOR MORE INFORMATION

BOOKS

Daly, Ruth. *How We Use Rocks and Minerals.* New York, NY: Crabtree, 2020.

Dickmann, Nancy. *How We Use Wood.* New York, NY: Crabtree, 2020.

Kington, Emily. *Future Energy*. Truro, UK: Hungry Tomato, 2022.

WEBSITES

Earth Science for Kids
www.ducksters.com/science/earth_science/
This resource has information on numerous earth science topics.

Kids Earth Science
www.kids-earth-science.com
Learn much more about Earth's resources at this detailed website.

Publisher's note to educators and parents: Our editors have carefully reviewed these websites to ensure that they are suitable for students. Many websites change frequently, however, and we cannot guarantee that a site's future contents will continue to meet our high standards of quality and educational value. Be advised that students should be closely supervised whenever they access the internet.

INDEX